The Spy Next Door

by Becky Cheston
illustrated by Nicole Wong

Harcourt

SCHOOL PUBLISHERS

Printed in China

ISBN 10:   0-15-377430-4
ISBN 13:   978-0-15-377430-0

Ordering Options
ISBN 10:   0-15-377149-6 (Grade 5 Collection)
ISBN 13:   978-0-15-377149-1 (Grade 5 Collection)
ISBN 10:   0-15-377889-X (package of 5)
ISBN 13:   978-0-15-377889-6 (package of 5)

2 3 4 5 6 7 8 9 10   0940   17 16 15 14 13 12 11 10 09

It happened during a summer week filled with boredom, a trampoline, and my eight-year-old brother, Nick. I had just returned from a month-long stay at Camp Brackenbee in Maine. After thirty days of fun—all with kids my age—I wasn't used to hours of backyard nothing.

My dad, a gymnastics coach, was sitting with us in the backyard on the hottest day of the year, or at least it felt that way. My brother, Nick, who was Dad's star gymnastics student, was spraying himself with the hose. I was leaning against the wooden fence, thinking about lunch.

"Dr. Ross's new lawn mower looks pretty nice," I said. Over the top of the fence, I could see Dr. Ross's house next door.

"Let me see," said Nick. He turned off the hose and walked over. "Dr. Ross still hasn't mowed his lawn. I bet it's because he's too busy—doing *spy* stuff!"

"Nick, the only spies around here are in your imagination," I said.

My brother and his friends had a new favorite game, called "Spies and Secret Agents." When his friends weren't around, Nick just made stuff up all by himself. I'd only been home from camp for a couple of days, and he was already getting incredibly annoying.

I looked over the top of the fence. The grass next door grew tall and brown, mixed with scraggly weeds and dandelions. A solitary sunflower was the only sign of life in the otherwise desolate yard. A shape at the window caught my attention. It was Dr. Ross. We gave each other a little wave. Dr. Ross, our neighbor for about two years, worked long hours at the hospital. When he was around, he and Dad liked to talk sports and politics.

"Is that him?" asked Nick dramatically. "Does he have that new walkie-talkie thing with him?" Nick bent down and flipped up into a headstand. "Definitely a spy," he said.

"Dr. Ross? He's just our neighbor," I said as I wrestled Nick to the ground.

"That's not what Derek and Miles and I think. Did you see his new gadget?" asked Nick. "It's a walkie-talkie!"

"You must mean his pager," I said. "Most doctors have pagers so that people can reach them any time. He is a doctor, remember?"

"Doctor Dangerous!" Nick was spinning such a wild story that when a voice sounded next door, it made *me* jump. "It's him!" Nick screeched.

"Cut it out," said Dad. He got up and came over to us. "Come on—get away from the fence. Why don't we practice some jumps, Nick? The Junior Regional Meet is coming up next month. Jeff—want to help me spot him?"

I groaned and dragged my bored self over to the trampoline anyway. My parents had bought the trampoline for me and spent a lot of time setting it up so that it would be safe. Before long, it became clear that I hadn't inherited the family gymnastics talent. I was okay with that—give me computers and a catcher's mitt any day. I could tell Dad was happy when Nick was old enough to go on the trampoline. It turned out that he was a natural!

I watched Nick race over to the trampoline, and somersault on. He took his usual warm-up jumps until he'd popped high up in the air. Then he tucked himself into a ball, spun around three times, landed, and spun the other way. As he straightened himself out, he shrieked. Then my brother slowed to a stop and flipped onto the ground.

"What's the matter?" Dad asked.

"In the tree!" Nick announced with great fervor. "Scary yellow eyes!" A tall oak tree grew in the back corner of our neighbor's yard. Half of its branches hung over our lawn.

"Come on, Nick." Even Dad was getting frustrated with Nick's antics. "If you don't learn to concentrate, you'll never be able to memorize a routine."

A shout came from next door. "Libby? Libby—here, kitty, kitty. Where are you?"

"Hey, Dr. Ross," I said. Our neighbor looked like he'd just finished an all-night shift at the emergency room. He still wore green hospital pants and a wrinkled white lab coat that was not exactly immaculate.

"Hi, Nathan," Dad waved. "Did your cat get out again?"

"I was bustling around the kitchen making a sandwich and didn't notice that the back door was open," our neighbor replied.

"Come on over!" Dad called out, beckoning him into our yard. "We've got iced tea. I'm sure Libby will turn up soon."

Iced tea sounded good, so I sat at the picnic table with Dad and Dr. Ross. With my hand around a tall, icy glass, I let their conversation—*midterm elections, the new recycling program, tires*—drone on in the background. When they got around to baseball, I'd tune in. The laziness of summer had finally started to sink into my bones when—

"Jeff!" Nick was pulling at my elbow. "*Jeff!*"

"Don't you have a secret message to decode or something?" I asked.

"Listen, this is important!" Nick said.

"Right," I said. "Well, let me finish my drink." I turned my attention back to my glass and found that the ice cubes were melting fast.

Across the table, Dr. Ross looked hot, too—and weary. Dad must also have noticed our neighbor's worried, distracted look. "Do you need us to help you look for Libby?" Dad asked him.

"I don't want you to go to any trouble," said Dr. Ross. "It's so hot out. Uh, should Nick be getting on that trampoline by himself?"

Dad and I turned and saw Nick climbing onto the trampoline. "What do you think you're doing, young man?" Dad shouted.

"There's a spy up in the tree!" Nick yelled. "I want to see him again!"

"If you don't get off, the only thing you're going to see is your bedroom door," said Dad.

Nick got down and glared at the picnic table. "Dad!" he whined. "I saw someone up there with binoculars."

Dad heaved a heavy sigh and swiveled my way. "Why don't you go do something with your brother?" he said.

I was about to whine, too, until I realized something. Maybe Nick was making up all this spy stuff because he needed attention. I *had* been away at camp for a month after all. A healthy dose of big brother would probably assuage his curiosity. I drained my drink and went over to calm him down.

"Want to do something?" I asked him.

Nick's eyes lit up. "Hey—you could be my sidekick or an evil scientist!"

"I was thinking maybe a game of catch." I gathered our mitts and a couple of baseballs from the back porch.

"Why do we always have to do what *you* want?" Nick asked. He folded his arms and glowered at me, so I had to tickle him.

"Tell you what," I said as he squealed. "We'll toss a baseball around for a minute, and then we'll see what happens." I walked past the trampoline and positioned myself with my back toward the big tree. "You ready?"

Nick stretched his mitt straight out, with the palm facing down. He was never going to catch anything that way. Sure enough, when I tossed a ball over, he swiped at it as if his glove were a butterfly net.

"Let me show you something, Nick." I walked over and turned his mitt so that the palm faced up. "Now let's try it." The next two balls smacked right into the curve of his mitt—and back out again. "Remember to squeeze your mitt!" I yelled.

Nick picked up the ball and bent his arm way back—
like little kids do when they want to put real power into
a throw. With his little body twisted back and his face
stretched into a grimace, he heaved the ball forward.
Predictably, it did not zoom toward the target—my mitt.
Instead, as his body swung in a full circle, the ball flew
wildly off into the air, hitting the tree with a loud *thwack*.

What happened next should not have come as a
surprise. I certainly should not have reacted the way I did,
embarrassing myself with a high-pitched squeal, and a
pathetic *Da-a-ad!* Maybe it was the heat. Maybe it was
the fact that Nick had been talking about spies for days.
Whatever the reason, what set me off was this: When
the ball smacked the oak, the tree—or something in it—
reacted with a bloodcurdling screech.

After my startled yell, I noticed that Nick was hiding
behind me. "What was *that*?" he asked, clutching my shirt.

Then Dad and Dr. Ross came running over. Our neighbor was shouting, "Libby? Libby!" He turned to us. "Where did that sound come from?"

Finally, it dawned on me—it was the cat that had screeched when the ball hit the tree.

"The tree!" Nick shouted, pointing. Reality had also dawned on Nick, who was no longer clinging to my shirt. "See? I *told* you. I *told* you something was up there," he said.

"You said a *spy* was up there," I said. "Why should anyone listen to that?" Meanwhile, Dad dragged out a ladder as Dr. Ross squinted up at the tree.

"I can't see her," Dr. Ross said.

"Nick? Do your thing!" said Dad. Nick put his helmet back on, and Dad boosted Nick onto the trampoline. Nick jumped the way he had when he'd first seen the "scary yellow eyes."

13

"There! On the middle branch!" Nick shouted, pointing.

I helped Nick off the trampoline while Dad steadied the ladder against the tree. Dr. Ross climbed up a short way to one of the branches that hung over our yard. "Here, Libby, Libby, Libby," our neighbor coaxed.

Finally, Libby, an orange-striped tabby, was purring safely in our neighbor's arms. Dad had put the ladder back in the garage. Nick was petting the cat. I was drinking another cold iced tea. Suddenly, a loud beep came from Dr. Ross's pocket. Nick jerked in surprise, grabbing my arm.

Our neighbor took out a small gadget and checked the screen. "I should call the hospital," he said.

"It's just a pager," I assured Nick. "No need to be so jumpy!"

"Actually," said Dr. Ross, smiling, "I'm glad you have a jumpy brother, and so is Libby."

Think Critically

1. What detail about Dr. Ross does Nick use in his story about his neighbor being a spy?

2. How does the author describe the sunflower in the neighbor's backyard? What does this image tell you?

3. How does Jeff, the narrator, really feel about his brother? Explain your answer.

4. At the beginning of the story, Nick says he sees something in the tree. Why does no one believe him until the end?

5. Do you think Jeff is a good older brother? Why or why not?

 **Social Studies**

Famous Spies Nick thinks that Dr. Ross could be a spy. Do research on the Internet or other library resource to learn more about famous spies and what they did. Summarize your findings.

 School-Home Connection Share this story with a family member. What were your favorite parts?

Word Count: 1,733